BUT I WON'T
GO OUT
IN A BOAT

Poems by
Sharon Chmielarz

For Linda,

Best Wishes.

Sharon Chmielarz

Oct. 23, 1996

NEW RIVERS PRESS

1991

Some of the poems in *But I Won't Go Out in a Boat* have previously appeared in somewhat different versions in the following publications: *Athena, Caprice, Concert at Chopin's House: An Anthology of Polish American Writers* (New Rivers Press), *The Dacotah Territory Midwestern Literature Anthology, Great River Review, Lake Street Review, Loonfeather, Minnesota Monthly, Ripenings, Slipstream, Slow Dancer, TAR* and *Visions: International Magazine of Illustrated Poetry* (Black Buzzard Review). Our thanks to the editors of these publications for the permission to reprint these poems here.

The author wishes to extend grateful acknowledgements to her editor, Vivian Vie Balfour, and C. W. Truesdale for their careful attention to this work. She would also like to thank Patricia Barone, Laura Littleford, Norita Dittberner-Jax, Carol Masters, Mary Kay Rummel, Barbara Sperber and Deborah Keenan for their help and encouragement in the manuscript's early stages.

New Rivers Press wishes to thank The Copenhagen Museum, Absalonsgade 3, Copenhagen, for its generosity in allowing the reprint of the photo "Prostitute in a Window Facing Holmensgade."

The publication of *But I Won't Go Out in a Boat* has been made possible by grant support from the Jerome Foundation, the Arts Development Fund of the United Arts Council, the Beverly J. and John A. Rollwagen Fund of the Minneapolis Foundation, Cray Research Foundation, the Elizabeth A. Hale Fund of the Minneapolis Foundation, the First Bank System Foundation, Liberty State Bank, the Star Tribune/Cowles Media Company, the Tennant Company Foundation, the Valspar Corporation, and the National Endowment for the Arts (with funds appropriated by the Congress of the United States). New Rivers also wishes to thank the Minnesota Non-Profits Assistance Fund for their invaluable support.

New Rivers Press books are distributed by

The Talman Company
150-5th Avenue
New York, NY 10011

Bookslinger
502 N. Prior Avenue
St. Paul, MN 55104

But I Won't Go Out in a Boat has been manufactured in the United States of America for New Rivers Press (C. W. Truesdale, Editor/Publisher), 420 N. 5th Street/Suite 910, Minneapolis, MN 55401, in a first edition of 1,200 copies.

In this part of the Dakotas a tree
is a freak in the grass.

for Mom
& the tree

CONTENTS

I. Half Sea

II. Half Land

*"The fulcrum of America is the Plains,
half sea half land"*

−Charles Olson

1
HALF
SEA

A fortune teller told me once
I'd die drowning,
    so I won't go out in a boat.
My Mother

DO NOT DISTURB

Do not disturb the sea in this house.
Do not make waves by leaping to fear.
Even a wake like a muskrat's through reeds
upsets the house Neptune, the angry
face behind trident and storm.

Do not think less of yourself, caged,
longing like the shipwrecked for a shore.
Even boats fail here, their hulks
quaver underwater among wrecks
of armchairs, tables, beds, shadowed

stumps in channels of light.

LIKE A CHURCH

Like a church on the North Sea,
the Berlin Baptist
stands on a hilltop,
a spare, big-boned house looking
over a sea of marsh and fields.

The walls run a good
fist thick
against the tides
of wind.
Two bars,
gun-barrel thin,
prop up the window frame.

Mullions square off the glass.
In the theology of rods they come
from four directions at once
to tame, bind and confound
the scope of the vision
as well as to divide
the immensity of the Great
Plains into parcels –

each pane, a handspan
wide. What light
falls in, remains,
the messenger from heaven,
underfoot among fixed benches.

On Sundays my grandfather comes to sing.
Pumped music rolls just over the tops of high notes.
His voice rolls like a breaker just under the crest,
all the way down to the end of a song and will not be rushed.

In the pause between hymns
you can hear the wind,
the sound of the farm,
the people I come from.
And its taste on the tongue is grit.

UNCLE HENRY'S SONG

The tune throbs
on waves
pumped by Uncle Henry
on the organ
in the basement.

Under his boot the bass
thumps. The tenor's
two notes float
up the stairs
into the kitchen

where we sit at the table,
our stiff raft stuck.
We're staring ahead to see what
Grandpa will do –
           he rocks
near the stove and ignores
the song of one who isn't
all there – Uncle Henry
keeps on pumping, the bars

keep rising past our chest, chins,
ears to float – "Oh, ah!" –
alone on a sea of doldrums,
alone on a hot, prairie day.

BLUE HARVEST

My memory's wrong; this part
of South Dakota isn't flat.
Under a landlubber's legs
the hills to the Missouri
roll like shipboards. And nestled
in the valley where lights
sparkle like hoarfrost
lies a house, fast asleep.
In rooms where the word 'love,'
or its touch, never wakened her, my
mother dreams whole harvests of love.
A blue haze drifts through the house.
I can't breathe – I run
through all the space in the world.
Do my legs even move?
I'm companion on the road
to telephone poles, masts
staked into the earth's hard
breasts. They pass messages
over lines without touching.
One wooden body to another
sends words of love and hate
writhing within the cable's lines.
The land sleeps on, in its coma.

READING RESPONSIVELY

I sat in church. I heard.
First the preacher read
from the pulpit. Then the people
answered from the pews.
Unbookish hands held blue hymnals.
Dark voices droned for light.
I heard little cries to abandon
all hardness in the heart
to the glimmer of love that shivers
under words in the Psalms.
'More to be desired than gold.'
'Sweeter than the honey or the honeycomb.'

But I was stubborn. I thought
what I'd learned in my father's house
worked better. By Sunday dinner
one hour later, I was back
practicing the rule of darkness:
to save the sweetness of light
you reject it. The way I reject
my mother, to save her brightness
from the jealousy of my father.
In the afternoon when I go out
I wear a hat against a light
hot and strong as irons.

AFTER THE DANCE

Mom was a pretty woman.
She couldn't help it if men
asked her to dance.
Dad was the disciplinarian.
When they got home
he hit her and washed her
dark hole out with soap.
He was a hard man,
the scissors I plunged at his back
couldn't go in.

WILD CUCUMBERS

A wild vine grows in the garden.
A snake choking my favorite tree.

Fear, seen but not heard, stands
by the fence, watching the vine

squeeze the limb as if nothing
is happening inside the house.

Finally, fear's father comes out.
To cool off his skin, he spades.

Fear's mother stays shut up
in her room. Tomorrow

the welts on her arms
will wax green.

A PLACE TO STAY

You lay in bed, Ma,
just like on "Queen For a Day."

We'll go to the store,
we'll watch out for Dad on the way.

You won't have to cook anymore.
We'll eat bought bread and butter

like a picnic on the sheets.
And no dishes to wash!

You can rock on the hotelporch
when Dad's on his shift

and when he's off
we'll all hide inside.

Us five in one bed?
Sure, it'll work,

two sleep down
and three lay up.

And us kids'll get jobs.
I'll sell Christmas cards, Ma,

door to door. Just
let's not go back —

shhhh! It sounds like *him*
coming down the hall.

HOMECOMING

At midnight the man comes home from his shift.
He pulls a chair up to his daughter's bed.
"Where's your mother?" The girl pretends
to sleep. Her braids sprawl across the pillow.
She is very near, behind the Hollywood headboard,
in the V-space in the corner, where she's slept
close to the girl for a week now. He asks again,
not nice anymore. "Where is she?" Slowly
she crawls out. The girl braces for her mother's
next beating but he pushes the chair back instead.
He glares at his wife. He goes in to their bed.
She follows in the still night. In the morning
they sit at their regular places around the table.

PLANNING THE MURDER

I go down to the cellar
to bank the fire
before going to bed.
I stoke the coal
just like he says,
three chunks will last
us through the night.
Only this time it's him
I push off the shovel,
his black head
rolls into the flames.
The fire leaps up,
he spits out my names:
bitch, sow, slut.
Red arms reach out
to pull me in,
to lie with him in hell.
I slam the furnace door shut
and go upstairs.
If he's not dead
he'll soon be home
to hiss at me in bed.

PINK EARS

Pig! Pig!
Feet scurry in the den.

A knifeblade flashes,
lightning in the dark.

Here's Yellow Tooth,
my father, panting.

Here's Pink Ears,
my mother, at the fire

with the apple
already in her mouth.

TAKING A SNOW BATH

It's simple when there's powder snow.
You find a barren space — a field of silence
between parents. You put on a cloak,
the color and sweep of bluejay wings
and then, so no one can see where it is
you're coming from, you sweep down —
cloak-tail, wing-sleeves gloriously
flying — Whoosh! You're in diamond snow.
You come up in whatever character you want.
I choose Bird, bachelor aunt. She ruffles
her feathers, sputters at a bath
when the kitchen's cold. With a long
blue shiver, she works the snow down
through oil and dirt in her wings
taking every grain she needs to come clean.
Then she flits her head and is gone.
The prints left behind are small
but the wingmarks, precise as knifecuts,
and the bad blood, pure.

PELICAN

Flapping off the dock,
a pelican
wobbles downriver,
lands like a soggy hat
tossed through a door. In air

it has nothing to do with hats or heads.
It glides over the river's mudbeds. It
cuts through the marsh's musk that
gags you as you stand still
watching

an ax split the water,
a scoop bring up a fish
squirming like a tongue
in the jaw's hot basin
and all the way down

the grasping gullet. A pelican,
carrying an almost dead
fish in its belly,
rattles its wings like feathered flags
and flops onto the dock.

CATCHING OUR LIMIT

Once my father
drove us over the Missouri,
out of Walworth County,
out to the Little Moreau
in Mountain Standard Time

to a land
where afternoons
are hot and dry and stink
like chickens scorched in boiling water,
where farmers use kerosene lamps
when lightning strikes the REA,
where mornings after a storm
rain and earth, branded together,
settle down and you can hear
land rolled over by silence.

It ate the sound of the motor,
the last creak from the chassis,
the bounce of the trunk lid,
the clack of tackle box and poles,
the worm can's thud, the crumble
of gumbo underfoot.

It spit out our two red bobbers.
They sidled together
in the Moreau's muddy water.

For one hour it caught us
and held us
in its net like fish.

GUIDE IN THE POWER PLANT

When I meet him, I recognize his name
and almost say, why I know you,
I heard your name often at home. You're
the dirty, rotten, son-of-a-bitch my dad
never could get along with at work.
But I don't. And he shows me around — we
look at the boiler, turbines, assort-
ment of wrenches, numbered and tagged;
walk up the steel stairs he dusts
in this three-story, prairie lighthouse.
I ask him a question. When he answers
his eyes shine like wet shit. He twists
his neck in the circle of his collar
like a cobra. Everything he says sounds
minced. His words are mice; they
slip in and out of his teeth.

THE LIGHTHOUSE KEEPER
DURING THUNDERSTORMS

A handsome man in workman's clothes,
a second Clark Gable I always thought
if Dad weren't so mean. And silent
like thunderclouds piling over the garden,
white mansions imploding, splendid rebels
who wouldn't be pushed around all day
by a hot, bossy wind, threats that glowed
and lit the dark wall of his profile. . .

At work thunderstorms were another story.
Summers Dad's switchboard went mad,
a thousand red eyes, blinking for light.
The steel stairs in the lighthouse clanged
as Dad ran down to the turbines cursing
his shift, the foreman, and us at home,
hungry bellies pinning him to a job he
hated.

We sat meanwhile at late supper,
five females under a sputtering lamp,
gloating over his failure
to keep the lamp over the table on.
Poor Dad! Against storms he was useless,
more like us. Then the lamp
would come on strong, we'd see the white
of our faces. One punch and light
was back in the belly of the room.

HAT TRICK

Under the hat's
brim, my dad's
face is
half
in light,
half in
shade.

Light
is shyly
in love
with her –
the woman
beside him,
my mother.

Shade
is angry
as ten men
scorned
by the bitch
beside him,
my mother.

The two sides
struggle,
pulled
by undertow.
Anyone close
gets sucked
in.

HIS EYE IN DARKNESS

1.
The Church

It isn't what it used to be when Lilah Hermann
was alive and deaconess. She kept the goats
from the sheep. Now they let anybody in –
you know that man that sang a solo this morning?
About believing in miracles? You bet he believes
in miracles. He used to work at First National,
stole sixty thousand dollars. The preacher
stood up for him in front of the judge and they
let him off! They made him Sunday School president.
What kind of a rot-gut outfit would let a skunk
like that be president? – I tell you it makes my
skin crawl. I get so nervous, I want to scream.
One of these days – if it takes ten years – God
help me, I'm going to get my gun and the good
Lord knows I'm going to use it.

2.
Neighbors

I told him I didn't want him leaning on my fence
when he watered his garden. (Garden, more like weeds!)
The wood's too old, the boards weak from his kids
jumping over to get their balls out of my garden.
All of a sudden he wanted to fight. He was like
a bull at my gate trying to get in. Then that sow,
that slut of a wife of his, starts screaming.
(If she were any good she'd have sent that drunk packing
long ago.) – It's too late now, but if only I'd
bought that house. If only I could talk to the old
woman who sold us this house. "You don't want a
corner lot," she said. She should have known about
neighbors. At 70 you'd think she'd have known.

THE BRUISE

He shows me the bruise on the back of his hand.
"From banging her up against the faucet," he says.
"It looks like a skunk." His laugh, a half-choke.
"Here's the nose, the head, the big bushy tail."
He points them out with his thick finger that's
shaped like mine, but I can't see the details
'cause he moves his hand too quickly away, as if
embarrassed by this purple blotch that's popped out
of history and, as a self-portrait, not worth seeing.

BABIES

In the new love triangle —
his wife clucking and cooing
to the bundle in her lap,
the great-granddaughter
whose cheekskin's eighty years
softer than his — he sits
alone at the point
of stony silence, counting
every rock in his contempt.

FALLING ASLEEP IN WINTER
WITH THE SHADES UP

The night he dies
this is what I'm going to do:
roll up the shades,
let out the dark,
lie on his bed
like an empty ladle
and with the room
sink into the snow's
strange light – a gray
pinched pink,
a stronghold
for shadows.
I'll watch them
leap up at his walls.

VARIATIONS ON A FEBRUARY MOON

Shadows in the yard,
moonlight on the snow,
windfall.

Moon's been sick with scarlet fever,
all her hair's fallen out.

Strands lie on cold pillows,
twisted as brushshadow on snow.

Moon glares into my window,
demands I leave my bed.

"See my ugliness,
my bulging eye,"
moon says.

Moon stops just short
of the tree's crown —
the nets, mazes, cages,
sticks, crooked houses,
lantern cases

moon slides through

taking with her
two planets and a star
in her travels from the east
to the west side of my house.

THRESHING GROUND

There must have been once
in the middle of the prairie,
alongside the river,
in front of the house
made of stalks and rush,
a man's broken cry
rising like a moon
roughshod over a woman's.

These cries would have come
from my father and mother,
long faces turned towards
the scrawny field behind them –
on the threshing ground,
a half-load of husks
in the black wagon.

They wail the harvest.
And the snow whirling round their heads.
And the chore, the marriage, pulled along ✓
to the end. They wail the seed, the small
seed of love they buried in spring.

AT HIS TABLE

Something was definitely rotten
in the kitchen. The enemy
smelled it, too,
and with his delicate nose
stalked it down
to the spot before the stove
where Cook stood
silent before his pointing
finger. "Slut!" The stench of curse
penetrated the house.
The children covered their mouths.
Cook held on
to the handle of the pot
which flipped
when he slapped her – for sauce
she'd spilled on a burner? –
then he sat down to eat.
Cook served. For 17, 18,
19 years everybody
breathed, everybody
ate the taste of rot.

FEUERPROBE
IN NORTH DAKOTA

Test By Fire.
A medieval torture.
If you were innocent, you lived.

It's an old German proverb –
what you don't have in your head,
you must have in your legs. But how
can you outwit or outrun the smart
long-legged English (who comes from
the Outside and speaks good American)
if you don't know his words
for the thoughts in your mind?
He drives up to your farm, ties
up your tongue, threatens your father
"Buy war bonds, or!" and when Dad won't
walks into the kitchen and rations
your mother's sugar. Anyway,

that winter, the eldest son, Ted,
(named after Big Stick Roosevelt)
and his brother, Karl, left the farm,
already dark at seven, for town
(Fredonia, North Dakota, 1915),
a comfortable distance from home
by any other means than barefoot
on snow, which is how they went
since the only thing a boy had to do
besides sleep on a starlit night
was make wagers to a brother in bed...

down cold stairs, past the waterpail
by the back door, out the yardgate
(CLOSE IT UP!), down the sectionline
to town – a darkened street they enter
like wounded cubs or clowns, hop-foot,
past the bank, elevator, cafe; closed,
but light ahead in the general store – they
stomp up the steps, throw the door open
on a room where the gay blades
lounge around on feedbags and Heuther's
counter with soda pop and chocolate.
Hoots, catcalls, names. "Ihr dumme Tiere,"
Heuther clucks. ("You dumb animals.")
They in turn rub their feet and roar
in pain – the cries small rooms extract
for the warmth of their enclosure.
(They never did go much farther.)

In his easy chair, shoes off, my dad
tells me this story, a practice run
in unloosening his tongue.

FACE

A shadow halves my face,
a black mountain
over a white valley,
a black streak
intersects the eye. . .

this is the mask ↙
of the terrible bird
children remember
when they're alone,

the bird with two minds
netted together,
beak and claw,
song and cry.

DOWN AT THE WATERTAP

Down at the watertap
five toads are sitting.
Along comes my mother
and feeds them cubes of bread.

Back in the kitchen
a loaf of bread is cooling.
Five crows fly through the window
and peck the halo-crust.

Can you recognize us?
The family? Toads, crows
hungry to eat
my mother up?

Her mask disappears
like the waning moon's
into the sky. We leave
the table feeling empty.

PLAYING HIS HEART OUT

for my North German uncles

That day we were trapped
between chartreuse living
room walls and the godly
cleanliness of afghans
saving sofa and chairs.

We were talking about
anything except Uncle Carl –
gone, how we'd miss him –
when Uncle Gus came down
the hall and stood in

the archway, his wiry
body strapped under a black
accordion. "Haven't played,"
he said, "for a long time."
So he played a waltz and I

squirmed in my chair under
the slow flow of grief. He
played a polka and I heard
my sister clapping lightly
for the mourner and his cheek-

bones, held over the keys,
red and high as Helgoland's
cliffs on the North Sea. Gulls
whirled and screamed around
the black load on his heart.

LYRE ON THE WILLOWS

Sister, being older
you have already taken the lyre
hanging from the willows,
and made yourself sing
over your son's grave.
So it must be true
when you tell me
out of the silence in an afternoon,
"We will lose Mom first."
This is not our will!
It is only fair
that HE should go first.
Something inside us
wants arms against this,
not words. We embrace.
What you've said
turns in my ears.
And you, tremble,
a bundle of sticks in my arms.
This is how wisdom informs
daughters of flesh and bone.

RABBIT

I went out of my house
to look at the moon.
Moon, hidden by trees.
But under the trees
in shadow, in grass,
I saw a small rabbit
like Dürer's, the same
throb in its throat.

2
HALF
LAND

[this land] . . . an ocean in its vast extent, in its monotony, and in its danger.

Lieutenant Colonel Richard Dodge
c. 1890

DURING THE BLIZZARD

Under the wagon bed
sits a young woman,
my grandmother-to-be,
spending the winter.
Cowchip and sod walls
keep out the full
blast of north wind.

And tonight
as a mean band of snow
hurls itself
against my city's walls,
the shadow of her small
room darkens
the fruit on my table.

TOWN AND BRIDGE

Long before the town was there,
a hut stood near the bridge
beside the cottonwoods that straggled up to the river
for water. In the hut the telegrapher
hunkered, taking messages. And the way
she shortened the river's name, gave the place
its name. With a name came the highway,
snaking through hay and wheatfields,
and the dusty street, then our house
and the boxelder in the front yard.
The town grew, preferring to stand off
from the river, away from the trees' shade,
preferring to sit and stew in 100° days
and grow stunted.

From our front step I could not see the steel bridge,
beams flashing like silver knives in white sun
over a thick tail of muddy water.
I remembered the bridge from Sunday car rides,
Dad driving !thrump thrump! over its sections.
At home on the steps I looked long
in the direction of the bridge that rose
to stretch over the back of the brown lizard.
Cross over it alone, I believed, and you were free.

HOUSE DRAWING

And here, I'm drawing a line –
to separate our house from heaven –
a roof for the box.

Under the line sits my father,
smoking in the living room,
anger glowing in the dark.
Dark because I've drawn no lines
for windows. Dark so I can't see.

Three more lines make a door.
And there! She
steps out. By drawing a hat
I make her look older. Now
she can leave the house for good.

In the two stubs drawn for her eyebrows
he comes out. I see my father,
the anger, the woman in my father.
I see I'm wearing his hat.

HOUSETALK

Always, after housetalk like
"I never loved you,
I never even liked you, I needed
a rock, I guess, and you were it,"

always rock sits there
in the room's hot silence. . .then
chatter – from what distant
garden? – the sparrows'

I love you, ground.
I love you, tree.
I love you, seed.
Sound of love burns

like ice in his straighttalk,
like spite in her throat –
the twin to his confession and
always lodged in the rock.

HOUSE IN A WHEATFIELD

In one of the house's terrible
storms, a window falls
flat over a field,
penning it into four sections.

Wheat grows up through jagged glass.
It runs like a cur, low, in half-
circles before the wind. Roots
check it on a million leashes.

One house-eye glares down,
like a man jealous of his daughter.
She buzzes with the insects'
blondlust. She sings to black

seeds of more catholic
grasses in the bottomland.
On the morning of her wedding
rooms slam. The bride's

face stings — this house
knows how to make its mark
burn. Like the sun
searing the house's shoulders.

41

LOVE DANCE

Into the heart of our house we go,
father, mother, sisters, we dance
like the Dacotah, around a tribal
pole, on a tether, attached by barbs
sunk deep into bared breasts.
Head back, throat taut, wrists tied
to partners – if one of them slips
all hearts feel the sharp pull –
the wonder of it! We go on,
hooked in pain around a totem,
in silence, showing
our teeth and blood
and pieces of ripped flesh.

FIRST SNOW

Mom sits by the living room window,
silent. She was waiting for snow
and got a visit from her daughter.
At first glance, they're the same
except when it comes, snow stays
longer, more like a friend.

Dad looks healthy in his chair,
rotund proof that God is male.
Mom looks old. She's given up
salvaging among the broken
decisions in God's cellar. She

turns from us both to watch
snow's coming – the suitor
who stands quietly outside,
inviting her out, bearing down
firmly on the door
without once using a fist.

TURKEY DINNER (For HIM)

5 a.m. The kitchen's
a coven for witches
under the sink's light.

We're up to put the bird
in the pan so HE
can eat at noon.

(He'll tell us how it
SHOULD be done
when HE wakes up at 10.)

We turn the turkey
(our deftness
looks nervous)

head south, ass
north (now
I sound like HIM.)

We shove it in
the oven, where
hours of heat

and basting, will make it,
as they've made us,
turn out overdone.

ALONG THE MILE LINE

One hundred starlings
bicker in the grove

near the farmhouse. I walk
into the abandoned

argument. "God-forsaken
place." "Woman, you're

killing me." Web-fences
snap across my chest.

HONEYSUCKLE HOME

*The roomful of blue roses comes
from a song in the Fourties; one
rose equals each time the lover
makes his partner blue.*

This is the home I'm going to leave.
This the small yard with its only tree,
my father's boxelder, whose huge-armed
shadows drum the honeysuckle bush
into its corner. See how bees
torment it with their craving, maybe
it needs to be tormented, maybe it doesn't. . .

This is my goodbye, one roomful
of blue roses from the song my mother hums
when she's sad. I think she'd rather
have them than his battering arms
around her. Maybe I don't understand, so
sweetly does this honey torment my teeth.

BLUE MASK

5 p.m. And no distinction
between the color of the sky
and the color of the snow,
the cold makes it one blue
icon, two bodies lying
lightly against each other,
never speaking.

5:05. You believe what you lost
was beautiful. Shadow time,
blue of the laudanum bottle,
the garden as it looks in winter
through smarting tears, a lingering
blue, like the hand about to choose
between the latch and the lock.

Assign perfection to it –
the walls of a belly,
the great day whale
rising from the ground.
Sky's heavy fin comes down
dipping below the surface,
stirring the limpid cold.

5:15. Eternal aquatint no longer!
The color grows darker, goes
faster towards the end, in debt
to good times and amber windows,
enhanced by stars in the flanks
of the animal moving swiftly
to reconstruct the black in night.

Prostitute in a Window Facing Holmensgade
c. 1900
The Frozen Image
collection of Scandinavian photography

HUSBANDRY

Dressed in white, for innocence
or death, she waits
clean as sugar in the window,
a young woman above the need
to get in and out of a house,

the big, black housedoor
below her window.
When it slams, her hand
skitters under the collar
around her throat.

She sits there, the splinter
in the eye of the house,
the bit of light lost
scurrying up the back staircase.
She sees what must be

the cameraman at the end
of the street. He would like
to come in. Her glance
moves over him, like a lean
hand over a doily and deftly

pins him in place.

STAR COLLECTORS

I knew a woman, a bank clerk,
who ironed every Sunday night.
Her room over a store
on a prairie mainstreet
reeked of heat, cotton
and starch. On one wall
a line hung with blouses,
a white harvest drying
among constellations of pictures,
movie star cut-outs,
white, toothy grins.
A galaxy spun around her
and the ironing board.

Her mom was dead.
Like mine.
After years she and I
have death in common,
the oldest and the bluest
bead in Christ's mass,
the culling of relief
from joy and pain,
the star whose light
stabs coldly in the night.
In our rooms it's the frozen
smile that keeps us
at loss for company.

FOUR SISTERS

The moon has risen
over our wandering in the woods.
Auriga, the charioteer,
the herald of winter,
is a house of stars
we'll never reach.

A two-headed man
lives in these woods,
one head a monster
with a fiery throat,
one head a father,
whose breast is locked.

Starlight on shovels.
We dig at nets
of roots. Roots
keep us down.
Roots keep us
from getting home.

PACKING THE LUNCHBOX

Where Ma slices the Thuringer
the countertop's scratched
like an old woman's forehead
from years under the butcherknife.

She covers a bowl of sauce
(she's canned) with waxpaper,
(he's left folded in the box),
snaps a rubberband around it.

If he doesn't swing his arms
it won't spill on the way —
five blocks — to work,
the powerplant beside the tracks.

For dessert, sugar cookies
(she's baked). Sometimes
a Pay Day or green grapes.
Not often. Boughten stuff

never lasts long around
this house — I love it.
"Will I ever have a lunchbox, Ma?"
"You don't need one. You come home for lunch."

Winter or summer his box is packed,
two sandwiches, cookies, sauce. No napkin.
His people never use napkins. If you never
make a mistake, you never need a napkin.

He's waiting. Ma snaps the clips on the black
lid shut and sets the box on the back doorstep
where he can pick it up without coming back
into the house — they don't say goodbye.

If something'd happen – if he got hit
by a carload of drunks, or if she
died of lightning strike, the black lunchbox'd
be the last thing passed between them.

A TRAIN PASSES BY

A train's passing by
the living room.
My father, mother and I
stop talking to listen.

"They've sanded the tracks," Mom says.
"Before, the whole house used to bang."

"Ka punk, KA punk," Dad sings,
"punk, punk, punk BANG!"

He pounds his chairarm.
Dust rises.

And I remember
how his beating her
used to sound.

"It's better now," she says.
"I hated that bang," he says.

A train's passed by.

Everything on the walls
– pictures, mirrors –
still shivers.

SPIDER WEBS, REMINDERS

Webs in the berry bush this morning.
On one of the threads a spider dangles
home. She holds the ant (she held all
night?) and in my shadow, eats him.

Sometimes the sudden appearance of
a spider flexing her spinnerets
or hoisting a pellet of a belly
over a red jewel of a berry

startles the picker. "Dirty poo!"
With a flick of a leaf, she
sweeps the minor horror away
and grinds its guts out with her heel.

Later, in her kitchen, which smells of
hot red pectin, she counts twelve
jars of jelly cooling on a shelf –
for the icy morning, when she cracks

the first wax seal. And her children,
feeding their toast with both hands to
their teeth, will grind
all her sweet rubies up.

MY BACHELOR AUNT

"The theory next that all we are are
stories, handed down . . ."
"Kin"
C.K. Williams

We were walking down the sectionline,
supper dishes done, wind died down,

a white stallion and a half moon
on the other side of the fence.

"Prince isn't used to strangers or women," Aunt Hilda
warned. "Don't go up to him alone." And when

I did, he bolted from my hand, galloped away
into the pasture, into the night's black cove.

Then Aunt Hilda told me how once
when he was young, Prince got loose.

"In the dead of night," she said,
"I heard this noise pounding round and

round the house. I looked out my window
and there was Prince in white moonlight.

"It was like a fairy story."
And her eyes glowed.

With great majesty she takes this
story down and hands it on.

56

MARRIAGE OF TWO OLD MEN

What are two lonely old men doing in this house?
They have no language in common,
only this mean and obstinate nature.
They refuse to tend each other's flock of geese
though they both want roast goose for supper.
What this marriage needs is a woman.
All the servant women in the house have died.
All the sluts have run away.
All the hardworkers have left for softer jobs
and the sisters have married ambitious men.
These two left are too cheap to advertise for help.
What will happen to this house? The geese?
What will happen to them without a woman?

THE ORCHARD, MARCH

These trees have the look of
unmanned machinery, black hoists
against a liquid sunset.

A boy in a red jacket runs zigzag,
ducking the branches, stumbling
on clumps of frozen apples.

When he's gone, the trees
return to the loneliness
of empty stages.

AT HER TABLE

Sometimes when I'm sitting at the table,
an ancient ease comes over my body.
Everything settles into light and shadow —
they come like ghosts into the room
to love the space still left.

The past is moonlit landscape,
childhood memories of home
more splendid when imagined
from these odd pieces left —
take this cup of longing. . .

Li Po! This was your
thimble full of wine.
Mom, this was our measure
of a perfect table. I set
the cup down like a vase

on a grave. "Now praise,"
says the angel, "Praise," from the shadows
around my shoulders. "Praise
has always turned this earth's
salt into sweetness in a mouth."

FIELDWORK

Around this field, a shore of shaggy woods.
The wild plum's in powdery heaven
when the tractor rolls like a tank
into low tide. Cold, choppy waves.
The disc grinds in. Chunks split,
pellets spray, dust balloons.

The color of a plowed field
changes like a river's
under skiffs of light –
blackwater, churned-up gray,
yellow sandbars.
The sweep of a knoll
is a flecked wing, pinned down.

One morning, 10,000 seedlings,
10,000 tiny wings
flutter on their stems. In rows
they make a rice-paddy green dash
straight for the blackbird's border –

a jealous thumbprint,
the plow's imprint,
holds the rows in order.

The rest depends on the elements,
on moderation from lovers
by nature immoderate.
Wheat is expected to grow
unruly, thigh-high,
into a honeywhite animal,
into an endless sea
you can wade through.

HOTELWINDOW

The birch, pines, road
into the woods –
a quiet arrangement
lies outside this window,
I'm near dark woods
but not lost in them.

The moon in eclipse
appears on the glass –
my face in reflection!
The penumbra's a rim,
light left from a dream, ↙
where I loved my dad.

SIXTH AVENUE WEST

Our house sat with three others,
old sisters hunched beside a bed
of gravel and dust, under a worm-
eaten canopy of six elms. This
my mother called our boulevard.

In September windows looking west
flared blind-red in the river's sunset.
Gates and housewalls held
under the transiency of smells – of
bonfires, wood, char and new

potatoes baked in leaves.
Networks of shadows, exiled from
branches by streetlamp, gangled
up the road past human shapes till
gusts of wind yanked them back

to elms again. The nighthawk
circled this edge of my mother's
pretentious misnomer. After summerheat
shadows, houses, road, elms, all
burn deeply together.

MARIE AND ELLA

When geese flock
and fly in strings, tangling
and untangling over the town
of small houses, over the widowed
and the one still living with the tyrant,
Marie phones my mother. "Ella,"
the widow says, "go to the door and listen."
With the speed of 80-year-olds on rag rugs
they open the doors in their neighboring houses
to hear the calls of the geese, honking
their way across heaven. "We're leaving.
We're leaving." Marie and Ella don't
close the door until the last
wisp of sound is gone. A sense
is tendered – they've been in
concert, these geese and women,
who've seen the world,
from both top and bottom.

MOON MOM

Are you in the moon, Mom?
I see its bright boat
flounder on waves
of clouds
and miss you again.
Is it your answer
when the boat slides
under? Please, moon,
glide out!

. . .she was always
afraid of water,
of falling under
into the dark.
Let me find her
as I used to
in the mornings;
her back turned
to me. Moon Mom,
safe at the window.

HALF LAND

"But I won't go out in a boat.
I'd drown," my mother said,
"a gypsy warned me once
so I spent my whole life on land,
married, had four children,
never any money. I drifted
in and out of memory, back
to Mama, her warm kitchen.
And when some nights I could've
died, I floated away
in sleep from the body
of the man lying beside me –
a good catch? HA!
A bullhead German,
the kind of fish
most women would've thrown
back in. But I kept him
to the end and now he
swims from the edge of my bed,
and I drown, alone, blood
flooding my brain . . . AH!
Is that what the gypsy meant?
HA! He's tipped me over in the boat
but, Mama! I swim all the way back home!"

THEY COME HUMMING

What is the keyboard
but a variation on a table,
a trough in ivory and ebony
for all the Hungry
to come and be
soothed by food's music –

> his head is bowed.
> Like the pianist at an old Knabe,
> Grandfather Gottlieb at the table
> flexes his thick, speckled fingers
> over the plate and begins to hum
> for the 15,633rd time,
> "Komm, Herr Jesu, sei unser Gast
> und segne was Du uns bescheret hast.
> Amen." Then he lifts
> fork and knife to the sausage and
> snaps the fried skin.

Eating is a reminder of
your link in the Great Chain of Being,
though Grandfather, der Gottlieb,
never knew life by that name.

> I do and I sit alone.
> Remembering the power
> in rings and chains
> I set no place at my table
> for old names, but still
> they come, down aisles
> in waist-high wheatfields
> towards my table, singlefile,
> out of groves of ashes,
> black-scarfed serfs
> with a ring in one ear,
> big-bellied, German-Russians,
> they come humming.

SHARON CHMIELARZ

author of *Different Arrangements* (New Rivers Press, 1982) grew up in South Dakota. She is a graduate of the University of Minnesota with a M.A. in education, and degrees in German and English. Chmielarz, a winner of the 1982 Minnesota Voices Project, and runner-up for both the Bush and McKnight grants, lives in North Minneapolis with her husband Tad, and cat, Fritz. In addition to teaching, Chmielarz continues to write, saying:

"I write poetry because:
a) "When I kept silence, my bones waxed old through my roaring all day long." (Psalms 32:3)
b) It reveals for me "the secret which is also the sacred." (Howard Nemerov)
c) It's better than bowling."